Rita is a fictional character inspired by a real Shetland pony that
sometimes escapes from her field in pursuit of new adventures.
She works at Park Lane Stables RDA, an award-winning RDA
(Riding for the Disabled Association) centre with a wide programme
of activities, including assisted riding, horse care, carriage driving,
equine therapy and hippotherapy. This centre helps thousands of
people every year with the help of horses and volunteers.
Help their activity: https://www.parklanestables.co.uk/donate

ISBN: 9798344616933

The real Rita, eagerly waiting to return to the field
after coming back from an adventure.

BOOK 5

Rita the Pony Explorer at Work

Rita and the Storyteller's Corner
Connecting Through Stories

Rita the Explorer is a small, black Shetland pony with a big, white patch on her back. She usually lives in a beautiful paddock paradise with her friends, Max, Tella, and Rocky. But on certain days, Rita works at a special stable, helping people with special skills.

On these days, she stays at the stables and enjoys spending time with the special people she helps.

One pleasant afternoon, while working at the special stable, Rita is paired with a girl named Mia. Mia loves to read but is a bit shy about sharing her own stories.

Mia has special skills because she is much more emotional than other people. Her superpower is that she can understand how other people feel. She is learning how to control her power without being overwhelmed by emotions.

Mia follows Rita as they walk through the park near the stables. They come to a cozy corner with a circle of benches and a storyteller sitting in the middle, ready to share tales with anyone who will listen.

Mia hesitates but nods, feeling a mix of excitement and nervousness. They find a spot close to the storyteller, who begins weaving a magical tale about faraway lands and brave heroes.

"That was wonderful," Mia whispers to Rita when the story ends. "I love hearing stories."

Rita smiles and nods. "Stories are powerful. They help us connect with others and understand different perspectives. Would you like to share one of your stories, Mia?"

Mia looks unsure but takes a deep breath. "Okay, I'll try."

With Rita's encouraging nudge, Mia steps forward and begins to share a story about a brave little mouse who goes on a grand adventure to find a hidden treasure.

At first, Mia's voice is quiet, but as she continues, she gains confidence and her story flows beautifully.

The listeners applaud and cheer
when Mia finishes, making her smile brightly.

As the sun begins to set, Rita and Mia head back to the stables. Mia feels grateful for the special time she spent with Rita and the valuable lesson she learned.

When they return to the stables, Rita's friends Max, Tella, and Rocky, who are also at the stables for work, eagerly gather around her.

"What did you teach Mia today, Rita?" Max asks.

Rita smiles and replies, "I took Mia to a cozy corner of the park where a storyteller shares tales. I encouraged her to listen and share her own stories, teaching her the importance of storytelling and sharing experiences."

Rita nods, feeling proud of Mia and happy about their special day. She knows that storytelling helps us connect with others and share our experiences, making every day a special adventure.

About the Author:

Marcel Olivé is a distinguished author and expert in Natural Horsemanship, as well as a horse and hoof care specialist.

With a deep passion for equine well-being, Marcel integrates horses into his practice as an Equine Assisted Facilitator and Leadership and Performance Coach. His extensive knowledge and transformational approaches have made him a respected figure in the equestrian community, where he continues to inspire and educate through his writing and hands-on work with both horses and humans.

Printed in Great Britain
by Amazon

52662516R00016